Highlights® Handbook

Phonics Fun
for Beginners

Compiled by Constance McAllister

Pictures by Edward King, Jerome Weisman and others

Short Sound of

The pictured clues stand for words that contain the short <u>a</u> sound. Say the words.

orange and

coat and

dog and

nails and

horse and

2

Long Sound of a

train

wave

vacation

The pictured clues stand for words that contain the long <u>a</u> sound. Say the words.

hammer and

ice cream and

shovel and

pencil and

chair and

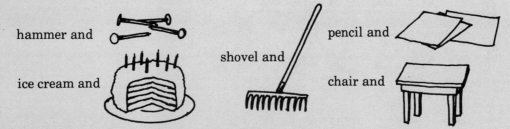

3

The Sound of b

Can you find **6** things in this picture that begin with the sound of <u>b</u>?

Initial Sounds

In each group, find the one that does not belong.

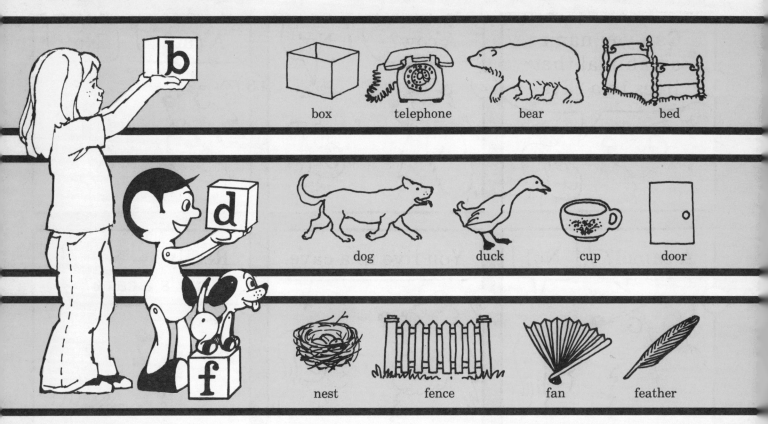

box   telephone   bear   bed

dog   duck   cup   door

nest   fence   fan   feather

When **c** Sounds Like **k**

Read the cartoon.
Notice that each underlined c has the sound of k.

When C Sounds Like S

Read the cartoon.
Notice that each underlined c has the sound of s.

Tongue Twisters

Each c in the sentences below has the sound of s.
Can you say each one three times quickly?

Dancing mice are very nice.
Princess Alice lives in a palace.
A cent apiece for celery, please.

The Sound of d

Can you find **5** things in this picture that begin with the sound of <u>d</u>?

8

Matching Initial Sounds

Look at each animal at the left.
Find one at the right that begins with the same sound.

mouse

duck

cat

fox

bear

bird

monkey

fish

dog

camel

9

Short Sound of e

Each word in the cartoon has the short <u>e</u> sound. Say the words.

The pictured clues stand for words that contain the short <u>e</u> sound. Say the words.

Long Sound of **e**

Each word in the cartoon has the long <u>e</u> sound. Say the words.

The pictured clues stand for words that contain the long <u>e</u> sound. Say the words.

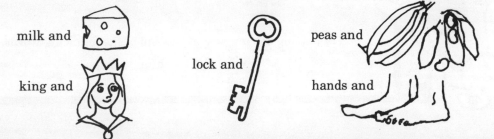

milk and

king and

lock and

peas and

hands and

The Magic e

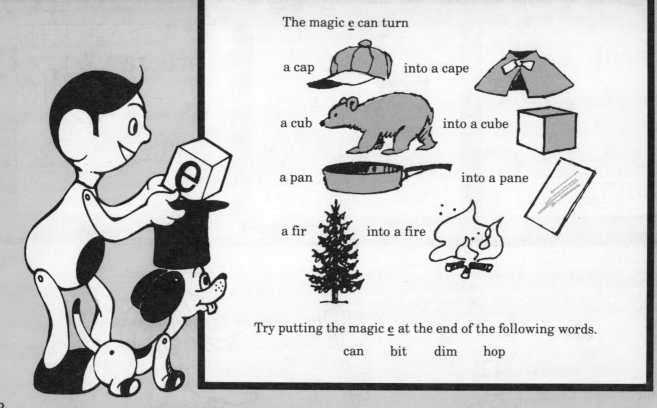

The magic e can turn

a cap into a cape

a cub into a cube

a pan into a pane

a fir into a fire

Try putting the magic e at the end of the following words.

can   bit   dim   hop

The
Sound of **f**

Can you find **5** things
in this picture
that begin with the sound of f̲?

When g Sounds Like j

Read the cartoon. Notice that each underlined g has the sound of j.

There's a genie in this bottle.

Really? Can it do any magic?

How do you think it fits in the bottle?

The Second Sound of g

Read the cartoon. Listen for the second sound of g (guh).

I can hear only one g sound in my egg.

I can hear two g sounds in my egg.

What kind of egg is that?

It's a goose egg!

In the big picture, find these things that begin with the g that sounds like j.

gingerbread

giant

giraffe

In the big picture, find these things that begin with the second sound of g (guh).

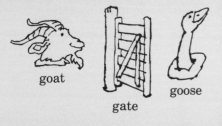

goat

gate

goose

The Sound of **h**

Can you find **6** things
in this picture
that begin with the sound of <u>h</u>?

Making New Words

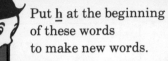

Put <u>h</u> at the beginning
of these words
to make new words.

air
eat
am
is
all

Put <u>f</u> at the beginning
of these words
to make new words.

it
or
act
ear
an

Put <u>b</u> at the beginning
of these words
to make new words.

us
old
in
each
ox

Put <u>d</u> at the beginning
of these words
to make new words.

ark
inner
ash
ate
itch

Short Sound of **i**

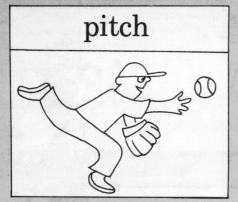

The pictured clues stand for words that contain the short <u>i</u> sound. Say the words.

gloves and

cow and

pumpkin and

cookies and

door and

18

Long Sound of i

The pictured clues stand for words that contain the long <u>i</u> sound. Say the words.

quarter and

cake and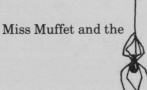

Miss Muffet and the

lion and

read and

19

The Sound of **j**

Can you find **5** things
in this picture
that begin with the sound of j?

Words Beginning With the Sound of **k**

Make up a story,
using four of these words.

kite

key

kettle

kitten

kangaroo

king

The Sound of l

mailbox

US MAIL

doll

lamb

Which word has <u>l</u> at the beginning?

Which word has <u>l</u> in the middle?

Which word has <u>l</u> at the end?

The Sound of m

Can you find **5** things
in this picture
that begin with the sound of m?

Making New Words

Put <u>l</u> at the beginning of these words to make new words.

and
east
ink
ate
end
it
ace
earn
ash
edge

Put <u>m</u> at the beginning of these words to make new words.

an
ill
eat
ice
ark
any
other
end
ask
ore

Words Beginning With the Sound of n

Make up a story, using four of these words.

necklace

nest

nail

napkin

needle

nickel

nuts

net

note

notebook

nurse

Each word in the cartoon has the short <u>o</u> sound. Say the words.

box

knock

pop

The pictured clues stand for words that contain the short <u>o</u> sound. Say the words.

can and

key and

pail and

shoes and

bag and

Long Sound of O

clover

rose

goat

The pictured clues stand for words that contain the long <u>o</u> sound. Say the words.

plate and

horse and

ladder and

door and

hat and

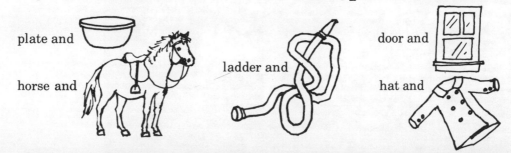

27

The Sound of p

Can you find **8** things in this picture that begin with the sound of <u>p</u>?

The Sound of q

Questions About q

When q is the first letter in a word, what will the second letter be?

How do you know?

The Sound of r

Can you find **7** things in this picture that begin with the sound of r?

The
Sound of S

Can you find **7** things
in this picture
that begin with the sound of <u>s</u>?

Making New Words

Put <u>n</u> at the beginning
of these words
to make new words.

ice
ear
arrow
ever
ow

Put <u>r</u> at the beginning
of these words
to make new words.

an
each
ice
at
oar

Put <u>s</u> at the beginning
of these words
to make new words.

our
end
ink
and
old

Put <u>p</u> at the beginning
of these words
to make new words.

air
in
age
inch
each

The Sound of t

Short Sound of **u**

brush

bucket

fun

The pictured clues stand for words that contain the short <u>u</u> sound. Say the words.

saucer and

chicken and

moon and

horn and

car and

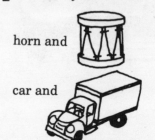

34

Long Sound of U

uniform

bugle

music

More words with the long <u>u</u> sound.

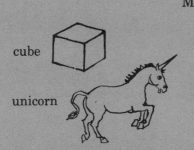

cube

unicorn

mule

United States

pupils

35

The Sound of V

Can you find 5 things in this picture that begin with the sound of v?

The
Sound of W

Can you find **7** things
in this picture
that begin with the sound of <u>w</u>?

The Sound of X

x-ray

ax

taxi

Which word has x at the beginning?

Which word has x in the middle?

Which word has x at the end?

The Sound of y

Unscramble the words
in each block
to make a sentence.

yelled
you
yawned.
and
Yesterday

yellow
Yes,
is
Yo-Yo
yours.
the

Say each sentence three times, as quickly as you can.

The Sound of **Z**

fez

zebra

puzzle

Which word has <u>z</u> at the beginning?

Which word has <u>z</u> in the middle?

Which word has <u>z</u> at the end?